**brunch**

RYLAND
PETERS
& SMALL

LONDON  NEW YORK

**Louise Pickford**

*photography by* **Ian Wallace**

# brunch

First published in Great Britain in 2001
by Ryland Peters & Small
20–21 Jockey's Fields
London WC1R 4BW
www.rylandpeters.com

10 9 8 7 6 5 4

Printed and bound in China

ISBN 10: 1 84172 197 2
ISBN 13: 978 1 84172 197 2

A CIP record for this book is available from the
British Library.

## Author's acknowledgements

Many thanks to everyone at Ryland Peters &
Small for their support, and of course to Ian,
who not only makes the food look fantastic but
is always on hand to taste my recipes and give
good, critical (and no-bias) advice.

## Notes

All spoon measurements are level unless
otherwise noted.

Ovens should be preheated to the specified
temperature. Recipes in this book were tested
with a fan-assisted oven. If using a regular
oven, increase the cooking times according to
the manufacturer's instructions.

**Senior Designer** Steve Painter
**Commissioning Editor**
Elsa Petersen-Schepelern
**Editor** Sally Somers
**Production** Patricia Harrington
**Art Director** Gabriella Le Grazie
**Publishing Director** Alison Starling

**Food Stylist** Louise Pickford
**Stylist** Antonia Gaunt

# contents

better than breakfast....

Like most people I know, I often find that breakfast these days is no more than a quick cup of coffee before dashing out to work. By mid-morning my taste buds are wide awake and I'm starving. This is the time of day I have to settle for a quick snack just to get me through to lunch. But at weekends it's a different story. At last there is time to enjoy a late start, followed by preparing something simple and delicious to eat. Brunch provides the ideal stopgap until the evening meal, but it's more than that. It is a great opportunity to indulge in all those foods we seem to crave the most. All our favourites – bacon sandwiches, waffles with maple syrup or eggs Benedict – make ideal brunch dishes. I only wish I had the time for such luxuries every day!

Preparing brunch for friends, a partner or family need not mean a hectic start to the day. Do what I do, which is to relax in bed with a great coffee and then to potter in the kitchen, getting things ready gradually and with minimal fuss. The recipes in this book enable you to choose dishes that can be either made in minutes or prepared the day before and cooked at the last moment. I've divided the recipes into sensible headings, so finding just what you fancy is simple and practical.

Most recipes serve 4–6, as unless you are planning a romantic breakfast in bed, you are more likely to be preparing brunch for a small group of friends. The ingredients can be halved or doubled as necessary. For any meal at any time of the day using fresh, quality ingredients is always important. I know we are all busy, but taking a little extra time to source good ingredients will produce even better results.

Most importantly of all, brunch is a fun meal. Get organized the night before so that on the day you can relax with your guests and really enjoy this little luxury.

# boiled eggs

## with asparagus soldiers

*Even as an adult I never tire of dunking toast into the perfect soft-boiled egg. Well, it's even better when you dip in asparagus spears. Remember that eggs need to be at room temperature before they are plunged into boiling water.*

24 thick asparagus spears
8 large free range eggs
sea salt and cracked black pepper
toast, to serve

**serves 4**

Tie the asparagus into bunches of 6 with string. Steam or boil for 3–4 minutes until just tender. Drain and keep them warm.

Meanwhile, cook the eggs in gently boiling water for 4 minutes, then transfer them to eggcups. Remove the tops of the eggs with a spoon and add salt and pepper to taste. Serve with toast and asparagus.

late

breakfast

*This is so yummy – a gooey, sweet, fruity porridge made with your favourite granola or muesli mix, soaked overnight in cinnamon-infused milk. Add whatever berries or soft fruits take your fancy.*

# cinnamon-soaked granola

## with fresh fruits

400 ml full fat milk

½ teaspoon ground cinnamon

2 tablespoons clear honey

300 g good quality granola or muesli, or homemade (see method)

200 g fresh fruit and berries

extra milk, to serve

**serves 4**

Put the milk, cinnamon and honey in a saucepan. Heat until almost boiling, then remove from the heat.

Put the granola or muesli into bowls, pour over the hot milk and let cool.

Refrigerate overnight and serve at room temperature, topped with fresh fruit and berries and extra milk.

**To make your own muesli:** put 200 g rolled oats in a bowl. Add 50 g oatmeal, 50 g oat bran, 50 g raisins, 100 g mixed dried fruits, chopped, such as apricots, figs, dates, banana and mango, 150 g mixed toasted and chopped nuts, such as hazelnuts, almonds, macadamias and cashews, with 2 tablespoons each of sunflower, pumpkin and sesame seeds. Mix well and transfer to an airtight container.

**To make granola:** put the oats into a dry frying pan over medium heat and toast, stirring, until toasted and golden. Repeat with the oatmeal, oat bran, nuts and seeds, in separate batches. Let cool and store in an airtight container.

# omelette
## *fines herbes*

6 free range eggs

2 tablespoons freshly chopped mixed herbs, such as chervil, chives, marjoram, parsley and tarragon

30 g butter

sea salt and cracked black pepper

a few extra chives, to serve

**serves 2**

*As omelettes are best eaten as soon as they come out of the pan, I tend to serve this for no more than two people. For larger numbers, simply multiply these ingredients accordingly.*

Put the eggs in a bowl, add half the herbs and salt and pepper to taste. Beat until runny and well mixed. Melt half the butter in an omelette pan until it stops frothing, then swirl in half the egg mixture.

Sprinkle with half the remaining herbs. Lightly fork through the mixture a couple of times so that it cooks evenly across the base.

As soon as it is set on the bottom, but is still a little runny in the middle, transfer to a warmed plate, folding the omelette in half as you go. Sprinkle with chives, salt and pepper. Serve immediately and repeat with the remaining ingredients to make a second omelette.

*There isn't much to beat figs straight from the tree, bursting with sweetness and a sublime flavour. Try to buy figs as ripe as possible for this dish. If they are unavailable, use other fruits such as peaches, apricots or cherries.*

# fresh figs
## with ricotta and honeycomb

500 g fresh ripe figs, about 8

500 g ricotta cheese, sliced

a piece of honeycomb or
4–8 tablespoons honey

**serves 4**

Arrange the figs and ricotta on a large plate and serve the honeycomb or honey in a separate bowl for everyone to help themselves.

# panettone french toast
## with coconut milk

½ vanilla pod

150 ml canned coconut milk

2 eggs, lightly beaten

25 g caster sugar

¼ teaspoon ground cardamom (optional)

50 g butter

8 slices panettone or other sweet bread

**to serve**

icing sugar, for dusting

blueberries

clotted or whipped cream

**serves 4**

*Using coconut milk instead of ordinary milk adds an exotic twist to this simple breakfast dish. For a slightly healthier version, serve with Greek yoghurt instead of cream.*

Split the vanilla pod in half lengthways and scrape out the seeds. Put the coconut milk, eggs, sugar, vanilla seeds and cardamom, if using, in a bowl and beat well. Pour the mixture into a shallow dish.

Heat half the butter in a large frying pan. Dip 2 slices of panettone into the egg mixture and fry until golden on both sides. Repeat with the remaining slices and serve dusted with icing sugar and topped with the blueberries and cream.

# waffles

## with maple syrup ice cream

*A classic brunch dish with a twist! If you don't have a waffle
iron, simply drop a ladle of batter onto a lightly greased,
heated frying pan and fry until golden on both sides.*

**ice cream**

500 ml double cream

250 ml milk

seeds from 1 vanilla pod

5 egg yolks

125 ml maple syrup

**waffles**

150 g plain flour

1 teaspoon baking powder

½ teaspoon
bicarbonate of soda

1 tablespoon caster sugar

125 ml buttermilk

1 egg, lightly beaten

75 g butter, melted

maple syrup, to serve

*waffle iron, lightly greased*

**serves 6**

To make the ice cream, put the cream, milk and vanilla seeds into a saucepan and heat until the mixture reaches boiling point. Remove from the heat and set aside.

Meanwhile, put the egg yolks and syrup in a bowl and beat. Stir in the heated cream mixture and return to the pan. Heat gently, stirring, until the mixture thickens enough to coat the back of a wooden spoon. Do not boil or the mixture will curdle. Remove from the heat and let cool. Freeze in an ice cream maker, following the manufacturers' instructions. If you don't have an ice cream maker, pour the mixture into flat freezer trays and put them in the freezer. Let the mixture partially freeze, beat to break up the ice crystals and return the trays to the freezer. Repeat several times – the more you do it, the smoother the end result.

To make the waffles, sift the flour, baking powder and bicarbonate of soda into a bowl. Stir in the sugar. Beat the remaining ingredients together in a second bowl, then beat into the dry ingredients until smooth.

Spoon a layer of the batter into a heated waffle iron and spread flat. Cook for about 1 minute until crisp and golden. Serve hot with a scoop of ice cream and a little extra maple syrup.

# blackberry buttermilk pancakes **with apple butter**

### apple butter

500 g cooking apples,
such as Bramleys

3 tablespoons soft brown sugar

a pinch of ground cinnamon

1 teaspoon fresh lemon juice

25 g butter

### pancakes

125 g self-raising flour

1 teaspoon bicarbonate of soda

25 g fine cornmeal

40 g caster sugar

1 egg, beaten

350 ml buttermilk,
at room temperature

15 g butter, melted

125 g small blackberries

oil, for greasing

### to serve

single cream

extra blackberries

**serves 6**

*Apples and blackberries are great together, and here a buttery apple sauce tops blackberry-dotted pancakes. Use blueberries or raspberries as an alternative.*

Peel, core and dice the apples and put in a saucepan with the sugar, cinnamon, lemon juice and 1 tablespoon water. Bring to the boil, cover and simmer over a low heat for 15–20 minutes until softened. Mash with a fork, add the butter and heat through, uncovered, until thickened. Set aside to cool.

To make the pancakes, sift the flour and bicarbonate of soda into a bowl and stir in the cornmeal and sugar. Put the egg, buttermilk and melted butter into a second bowl and beat until mixed. Stir the mixture into the dry ingredients to form a smooth, thick batter. Fold in the blackberries.

Heat a heavy based, non-stick frying pan until hot, brush lightly with oil and pour in a little of the batter to form a small pancake. Cook for 2 minutes until bubbles appear over the surface. Flip and cook for a further 1 minute until cooked through. Keep the cooked pancakes warm in a low oven while cooking the rest.

Serve the pancakes topped with apple butter, a little cream and blackberries.

# bagels

## with smoked salmon and wasabi crème fraîche

*A classic American brunch dish given a modern twist with Japanese wasabi paste (horseradish) added to the crème fraîche.*

4 plain bagels

200 g crème fraîche

2–3 teaspoons wasabi paste

freshly ground black pepper

250 g smoked salmon

**to serve**

chopped chives (optional)

lemon wedges (optional)

**serves 4**

Cut the bagels in half and toast lightly on both sides. Put the crème fraîche and wasabi paste in a bowl and beat until evenly mixed. Add black pepper to taste.

Spread 4 bagel halves with the wasabi mixture. Top with the smoked salmon and chives, if using, then add the remaining bagel halves. Serve with lemon wedges, if using.

classic brunch

# eggs benedict

*I usually fry the Parma ham so it becomes really crisp, adding a lovely texture to the creamy sauce and egg yolks. Try substituting smoked salmon for the ham or, for a vegetarian version, replace the ham with wilted spinach.*

4 large slices of Parma ham

4 free range eggs

4 plain English muffins

**hollandaise sauce**

250 g unsalted butter

3 free range egg yolks

2 tablespoons water

1 teaspoon freshly squeezed lemon juice

sea salt and cracked black pepper

**serves 4**

To make the hollandaise sauce, put the butter in a small saucepan and melt gently over a very low heat, without letting it brown. Put the egg yolks, water and lemon juice into a blender and process until frothy. With the blade turning, gradually pour in the melted butter in a steady stream until the sauce is thickened and glossy. Transfer the sauce to a bowl set over a saucepan of hot water. Cover and keep the sauce warm.

Grill or fry the slices of Parma ham until really crisp and keep them warm in a low oven. To poach the eggs, bring a saucepan of lightly salted water to the boil. Add 1 tablespoon vinegar, preferably distilled, and reduce to a gentle simmer. Swirl the water well with a fork and crack 2 eggs into the water. Cook for 3 minutes, remove with a slotted spoon and repeat with the remaining 2 eggs.

Meanwhile, toast the muffins whole and top each with a slice of crispy ham. Put the poached eggs on top of the ham. Spoon over the hollandaise, sprinkle with salt and pepper and serve at once.

**Note:** to poach eggs in advance, follow the directions above and as soon as the eggs are cooked, plunge them into iced water. Just before serving, return them to a saucepan of gently boiling water for a few seconds to heat through.

# mushrooms on toast

## with melted cheese

*Large, juicy field mushrooms need little embellishment – just a slice of cheese and a hint of sweetness from the brioche.*

8 large portobello mushrooms, wiped and trimmed

125 g butter

4 slices of brioche or granary bread

125 g Taleggio cheese

sea salt and freshly ground black pepper

**serves 4**

Melt the butter in a pan, add the mushrooms and cook for 8–10 minutes, until golden and beginning to give up their juices. Add salt and pepper to taste.

Meanwhile, toast the brioche slices on both sides under a grill. Spoon over the mushrooms and their juices and top with the Taleggio. Return the topped brioche to the grill for a few seconds, so that the cheese just begins to melt. Serve at once.

1 small gammon knuckle, soaked overnight in cold water

800 g canned borlotti beans, drained and rinsed

1 garlic clove, crushed

1 onion, finely chopped

450 ml vegetable stock

300 ml passata

2 tablespoons molasses or black treacle

2 tablespoons tomato purée

1 tablespoon soft dark brown sugar

1 tablespoon Dijon mustard

1 tablespoon red wine vinegar

freshly ground black pepper

toast, to serve

**serves 6**

# homemade baked beans

Drain the soaked gammon knuckle, wash and pat dry. Put into a large, flameproof casserole.

Add the beans and all the remaining ingredients to the casserole. Cover and bring slowly to the boil on top of the stove, then transfer to a preheated oven at 170°C (325°F) Gas 3 and bake for 1½ hours. Remove the lid and cook for a further 30–45 minutes, until the sauce is syrupy.

Remove the gammon to a board and cut any meat into slices. Put the toast onto serving plates, top with the beans and gammon and serve hot.

*Soaking the gammon overnight removes excess salt from the meat. Traditionally, dried beans would have been used in this dish (often called Boston baked beans) but using canned reduces the cooking time by two-thirds.*

# hash browns

## with sausages and oven roasted tomatoes

750 g floury potatoes, such as desirée, peeled and diced

50 g butter

1 large onion, finely chopped

12 good quality sausages

2 tablespoons olive oil

500 g cherry tomatoes, on the vine

1 tablespoon balsamic vinegar

sea salt and freshly ground black pepper

**serves 4**

Cook the potatoes in a large saucepan of lightly salted, boiling water for 10–12 minutes, until almost cooked through. Drain well and mash roughly.

Melt the butter in a large non-stick frying pan and gently fry the onion for 15 minutes, until soft and golden. Add the potatoes and salt and pepper. Cook, stirring and mashing the potatoes occasionally, for 15–20 minutes, until well browned and crispy around the edges.

Meanwhile, put the sausages in a roasting tin, drizzle with half the oil and roast on the middle shelf of a preheated oven at 200°C (400°F) Gas 6 for 25 minutes.

Once the sausages are in the oven, put the tomatoes, still on the vine, in an oven dish. Drizzle with the remaining oil and put on the top shelf of the oven after the sausages have been cooking for 5 minutes. Cook for 15 minutes, drizzle over the balsamic vinegar and cook for a final 5 minutes.

Spoon the hash browns onto plates and top with the sausages, tomatoes and their juices.

*A good breakfast for when you're feeling a little the worse for wear – great comfort food.*

# kedgeree

## with tea-smoked salmon

*Tea-smoked salmon replaces the more traditional smoked haddock in this version of the classic English breakfast dish.*

40 g butter

1 onion, finely chopped

250 g basmati rice

1 tablespoon curry paste

4 cardamom pods, crushed

1 cinnamon stick, crushed

1 teaspoon ground turmeric

600 ml fish or vegetable stock

**tea-smoked salmon**

500 g salmon fillet

8 tablespoons rice

8 tablespoons tea leaves

8 tablespoons soft brown sugar

sea salt and freshly ground black pepper

**to serve**

2 hard-boiled free range eggs, peeled and quartered

1 tablespoon chopped fresh chives

1 tablespoon chopped fresh parsley

**serves 6**

Melt the butter in a saucepan, add the onion and fry gently for 5 minutes. Add the rice, curry paste and spices, stir once, then add the stock. Bring to the boil, cover and simmer over a very low heat for 20 minutes.

Meanwhile, to smoke the salmon, cut the fillet into 4 equal pieces and sprinkle with salt and pepper. Line a wok with a sheet of foil and put the rice, tea leaves and sugar in the bottom. Arrange a rack over the top. Cover and heat for 5–8 minutes, until the mixture starts smoking. Slide the fish fillets, skin side down, onto the rack, cover and smoke over a high heat for 4 minutes. Remove the wok from the heat but leave undisturbed for a further 3 minutes. Remove the fish and keep it warm.

Skin and flake the salmon into large pieces and add to the spiced rice. Add salt and pepper and mix briefly with a fork. Cover and leave for 5 minutes. Serve topped with the egg quarters and sprinkled with the chopped herbs.

*Caesar salad is a classic brunch dish and here the original is jazzed up with fresh crabmeat. You will need brown and white crabmeat and if you are using whole, cooked crab, you will need one that weighs about 1 kg.*

# crab caesar

4 thick slices of white bread, crusts removed

2 free range egg yolks

2 teaspoons Dijon mustard

2 tablespoons freshly squeezed lemon juice

a pinch of cayenne pepper

200 ml extra virgin olive oil

3 cos lettuce hearts

350 g fresh mixed crabmeat

12 anchovy fillets in oil, drained

sea salt and freshly ground black pepper

vegetable oil, for frying

**serves 4**

To make croutons, cut the bread into cubes. Put enough oil in a frying pan to cover the base, then heat until hot. Add the bread cubes and fry, stirring constantly, until evenly golden and crisp. Drain on kitchen paper.

Put the egg yolks, mustard, lemon juice and cayenne pepper in a bowl and whisk until blended. Gradually whisk in the oil in a steady stream, until the sauce is the consistency of a thin mayonnaise. Add salt and pepper to taste. Remove a third of the sauce and reserve for another dish. (Cover it with clingfilm and refrigerate for up to 3 days.)

Tear the lettuce into bite-sized pieces and put in a large bowl. Add the croutons and white crabmeat. Add the brown crabmeat to the remaining two-thirds of the sauce and mix well.

Pour the crabmeat sauce over the salad and toss gently to mix. Top with the anchovy fillets and serve.

early lunch

# blt tortilla panini

*Large flour tortillas make perfect wraps – these are filled and then cooked on a stove-top grill pan for a yummy toasted sandwich.*

16 slices of smoked pancetta or bacon

4 large flour tortillas

4 ripe tomatoes, sliced

125 g Gruyère cheese, sliced

125 g crisp lettuce, shredded

4 tablespoons mayonnaise

sea salt and freshly ground black pepper

**serves 4**

Put the pancetta or bacon slices in a dry frying pan over medium heat and cook gently until golden and crispy.

Put the tortillas on a work surface and arrange 4 pancetta slices down the centre of each one. Top with the tomatoes, cheese, lettuce and mayonnaise, lightly sprinkling with salt and pepper as you go.

Fold the edges over to form a wrap and cook seam side down in a hot stove-top grill pan for 2 minutes. Flip and cook for a further 2 minutes on the second side. Serve hot.

4 large portobello mushrooms, trimmed

1 tablespoon extra virgin olive oil

4 large ciabatta rolls

sea salt and cracked black pepper

mixed salad, to serve

**shallot jam**

1 tablespoon extra virgin olive oil

125 g shallots, thinly sliced

2 tablespoons redcurrant jelly

1 tablespoon red wine vinegar

**garlic mayonnaise**

1 free range egg yolk

1 garlic clove, crushed

1 teaspoon freshly squeezed lemon juice

a pinch of sea salt

150 ml light olive oil

**serves 4**

*You can keep leftover mayonnaise covered and refrigerated for up to three days.*

# mushroom burgers
## with shallot jam and garlic mayonnaise

To make the jam, heat the oil in a small frying pan and cook the shallots for 15 minutes. Add the redcurrant jelly, vinegar and 1 tablespoon water. Cook for a further 10–15 minutes, until reduced and thickened. Add salt and pepper to taste and let cool.

To make the mayonnaise, put the egg yolk, garlic, lemon juice and salt in a bowl and whisk until blended. Gradually whisk in the oil, a little at a time, until thickened and glossy.

Brush the mushrooms all over with the oil and sprinkle with salt and pepper. Add to a non-stick frying pan and cook for 4–5 minutes each side. Cut the ciabatta rolls in half and toast on a preheated stove-top grill pan. Put the mushrooms on 4 of the toasted ciabatta halves and top with shallot jam, mayonnaise and the remaining ciabatta halves. Serve with a mixed salad.

*The eggs are fried quickly in very hot oil, giving them an almost lacy look and lovely crisp texture.*

# frazzled eggs
## with smoked gammon

2 tablespoons wholegrain mustard

1 tablespoon clear honey

4 smoked gammon steaks

2 tablespoons extra virgin olive oil

4 large free range eggs

sea salt and cracked black pepper

tomato ketchup and hash browns (page 29), to serve (optional)

**serves 4**

Mix the mustard and honey together and brush over the gammon steaks. Grill for 2–3 minutes on each side, until cooked through. Cover loosely with foil and keep them warm while cooking the eggs.

Heat the oil in a frying pan until really hot. Add the eggs, 2 at a time, and cook until the whites are bubbly and crispy looking. Put an egg on top of each gammon steak. Sprinkle with salt and pepper and serve with tomato ketchup and some hash browns, if using.

# creamy eggs
## with goats' cheese

12 free range eggs

100 ml single cream

2 tablespoons chopped fresh marjoram

50 g butter

200 g goats' cheese, diced

a handful of nasturtium flowers, torn (optional)

sea salt and cracked black pepper

toasted walnut bread, to serve

**serves 4**

*Stirring a little creamy goats' cheese into lightly scrambled eggs transforms a simple dish into a delicious light lunch. The nasturtium flowers are optional, but they do add a delightful flash of colour as well as a delicate peppery flavour.*

Beat the eggs in a bowl with the cream, marjoram and a little salt and pepper. Melt the butter in a non-stick saucepan, add the eggs and stir over a low heat until the eggs are beginning to set.

Stir in the goats' cheese and continue to cook briefly, still stirring, until the cheese melts into the eggs. Add the nasturtium flowers, if using, and spoon onto the toast. Serve immediately.

# charred asparagus and herb frittata
## with smoked salmon

*Charring the asparagus spears on a stove-top grill pan intensifies their flavour and adds a smokiness to the frittata.*

250 g asparagus spears

1 tablespoon extra virgin olive oil

6 free range eggs

4 spring onions, finely chopped

2 tablespoons chopped fresh herbs, such as tarragon, dill and mint

50 g ricotta

15 g butter

250 g smoked salmon

sea salt and cracked black pepper

**to serve**

crème fraîche

lemon wedges

**serves 4**

Trim the asparagus and toss with the oil and a little salt and pepper. Heat a stove-top grill pan until hot, add the asparagus and cook for 3–4 minutes, turning until evenly charred. Set aside to cool.

Put the eggs in a bowl and beat until evenly mixed. Stir in the spring onions, herbs and ricotta. Add salt and pepper to taste.

Melt the butter in a large non-stick frying pan, add the egg mixture and swirl to the edge of the pan. Arrange the asparagus spears over the top and cook for 3–4 minutes until set underneath.

Put briefly under a hot grill to cook the surface, then let cool to room temperature.

Cut into slices and serve with the smoked salmon, crème fraîche and lemon wedges.

# salmon and sweet potato fishcakes

500 g salmon fillets

1 tablespoon olive oil

500 g sweet potatoes, peeled and cubed

4 spring onions, finely chopped

1 small garlic clove, crushed

grated zest and juice of ½ lemon

50 g fine cornmeal

sunflower oil, for frying

sea salt and cracked black pepper

green salad, to serve

**lemon and rosemary mayonnaise**

leaves from 1 sprig of fresh rosemary

½ teaspoon sea salt

2 free range egg yolks

1 teaspoon Dijon mustard

300 ml olive oil

1–2 tablespoons freshly squeezed lemon juice

**serves 4**

*I love fishcakes, and these, made with sweet potatoes, are a particular favourite.*

Put the salmon fillets on a sheet of foil and drizzle with the oil. Wrap the foil loosely around the salmon and bake in a preheated oven at 200°C (400°F) Gas 6 for 20–25 minutes. Remove from the oven and leave until cold. Flake the flesh with a fork, reserving any juices from the parcel.

Cook the potatoes in lightly salted, boiling water for 15 minutes. Drain well, return to the saucepan and dry out briefly over a low heat. Mash coarsely and set aside to cool.

Add the fish with the juices, spring onions, garlic, lemon zest and juice to the cooled potatoes. Add salt and pepper to taste and mix well. Shape into 8 small fishcakes and refrigerate for 30 minutes.

To make the mayonnaise, grind the rosemary leaves and salt to a powder with a mortar and pestle. Put in a food processor with the egg yolks and mustard and blend briefly. With the motor running, gradually add the oil through the funnel until thickened and glossy. Add lemon juice to taste.

Coat the fishcakes with cornmeal. Put enough oil to cover the bottom in a frying pan and heat until hot. Add the fishcakes and fry for 4–5 minutes on each side until golden. Serve with the mayonnaise and a green salad.

*A simple fruit compote that I like to serve slightly warm. You can use nectarines instead of peaches, plus whatever berries you fancy.*

# warm compote
## with peaches, apricots and blueberries

2 oranges
3 ripe peaches, sliced
8–12 apricots, halved
175 g blueberries
25 g caster sugar
1 cinnamon stick
Greek yoghurt, to serve

**serves 4**

Peel the rind from 1 of the oranges, removing only the zest and not the bitter white pith. Cut the rind into thin strips and put in a shallow saucepan. Squeeze the juice from both oranges and add to the saucepan.

Add the fruit, sugar and cinnamon stick to the pan and heat gently until the sugar dissolves. Cover and simmer gently for 4–5 minutes, until the fruits are softened.

Remove from the heat. Serve warm with Greek yoghurt.

sweet things

# baby custard tarts
**with cardamom coffee**

300 g sweet shortcrust pastry, thawed if frozen

300 ml milk

75 g caster sugar

1 teaspoon vanilla extract

2 egg yolks

1 whole egg

½ tablespoon cornflour

ground cinnamon, to dust

**cardamom coffee**

3 cardamom pods

4 tablespoons espresso coffee beans

7.5 cm biscuit cutter

two 12-hole mini muffin sheets, 5 cm across and 2 cm deep baking beans or rice

**makes 24**

*This recipe is inspired by the little custard tarts ('pasteis de nata') found all over Portugal. A shot of strong, spiced coffee makes a perfect accompaniment.*

Roll out the pastry on a lightly floured surface. Using a biscuit cutter, stamp out 24 rounds. Press the rounds carefully into the muffin sheets, lightly prick the pastry bases and line each with a circle of baking parchment.

Fill the cases with baking beans (or rice if you don't have baking beans) and bake in a preheated oven at 200°C (400°F) Gas 6 for 5 minutes. Remove the paper and beans and return to the oven for a few more minutes to crisp. Set aside and reduce the oven temperature to 150°C (300°F) Gas 2.

Meanwhile, to make the filling, put the milk, sugar and vanilla extract in a saucepan and bring to the boil. Simmer until reduced by about half.

Put the egg yolks, whole egg and cornflour in a bowl and beat well. Gradually beat in the vanilla milk. Pour the mixture into the pastry cases and bake for 10 minutes, until the surface of the custard is glossy and the centres are just set. Set aside until cold.

To make the coffee, remove the seeds from the cardamom pods and grind with the coffee beans, in a coffee grinder. Use the ground cardamom coffee to make espresso in the normal way.

Dust the tarts with cinnamon and serve with a small cup of the spiced coffee.

# pecan and chocolate muffins

*I use good quality dark chocolate, chopped up, rather than chocolate chips, as it has a much better flavour and texture.*

250 g self-raising flour

1 teaspoon baking powder

75 g pecan nuts, finely ground

125 g soft brown sugar

1 egg

50 ml maple syrup

250 ml milk

50 g butter, melted

100 g dark chocolate, coarsely chopped into very small pieces

chopped pecans, to decorate

*one 12-hole muffin tray, lined with paper cases*

**makes 12**

Sift the flour and baking powder into a bowl and stir in the pecan nuts and sugar. Put the egg, maple syrup, milk and melted butter into a second bowl and beat well. Beat into the dry ingredients, then fold in the chocolate pieces.

Spoon the mixture into the paper cases, sprinkling the surface with extra chopped pecans.

Bake in a preheated oven at 200°C (400°F) Gas 6 for 18–20 minutes, until risen and golden. Cool on a wire tray and serve warm.

# walnut cake

## with coffee syrup

*Coffee and walnuts are wonderful together, and this is a perfect way to combine them. Drizzling the nutty sponge with a spiced coffee syrup leaves it deliciously moist and gooey.*

6 eggs, separated

175 g caster sugar

175 g walnuts, finely ground

75 g day-old breadcrumbs

whipped cream, to serve

**coffee syrup**

300 ml strong black coffee

100 g caster sugar

3 star anise

*23 cm springform cake tin, greased and base-lined*

**serves 8**

Put the egg yolks into a large bowl, add 125 g of the sugar and whisk until pale. Stir in the ground walnuts and breadcrumbs. (The mixture will be very stiff at this stage.)

Whisk the egg whites in a separate bowl until soft peaks form, then gradually whisk in the remaining sugar. Stir a large spoonful into the cake mixture, then fold in the rest until evenly mixed. Spoon into the prepared cake tin and bake in a preheated oven at 180°C (350°F) Gas 4 for 35–40 minutes, until risen and springy to the touch.

Meanwhile, put the coffee, sugar and star anise in a saucepan. Heat until the sugar dissolves, then boil for 5–6 minutes until syrupy. Cool slightly.

Using a cocktail stick, spike the cake all over the surface and drizzle with half the syrup. Set aside to cool slightly. Serve the cake still warm with lightly whipped cream and the remaining coffee syrup spooned around it in a pool.

# sweet bruschetta

## with quince-glazed figs

*Quince paste is available from specialist food stores, or alternatively use redcurrant jelly or raspberry jam.*

2 tablespoons quince paste

25 g butter

2 tablespoons port

12 ripe figs, halved

4 slices of brioche loaf or challah

icing sugar and cinnamon, to dust

Greek yoghurt, to serve

**serves 4**

Put the quince paste, butter and port in a saucepan and heat gently until melted. Arrange the figs, cut side up, in an ovenproof dish. Spoon over the port mixture, making sure the surface of each fig is well covered.

Put under a hot grill and cook for 3–5 minutes, until the figs are caramelized and heated through.

Meanwhile, toast the brioche or challah on a stove-top grill pan. Transfer to heated serving plates and sprinkle immediately with icing sugar and cinnamon. Top with the figs and serve with Greek yoghurt.

# iced bloody mary

*Wonderful, with or without a hangover!*

300 ml iced Stolichnaya or Absolut vodka

600 ml tomato juice

juice of 1 lemon

4 tablespoons Worcestershire sauce

½–1 teaspoon Tabasco sauce

600 ml crushed ice

**serves 2–3**

Put all the ingredients in a blender and pulse briefly to a coarse purée. Transfer to a bowl and freeze for about 1–1½ hours, until slushy and slightly icy. Using an electric or a balloon whisk, beat briefly to soften. The mixture should be creamy but just liquid enough to pass through a straw. Transfer to glasses and serve with short straws.

drinks

# iced coffee

*This iced coffee can also be served black.*

600 ml freshly made espresso coffee
sugar (optional)
milk

**serves 2**

Chill the freshly made espresso coffee, sweetened with sugar, if using. Pour into chilled glasses, adding a few ice cubes. Top up with a little milk and serve.

# mocha affogato

*'Affogato' is Italian for 'drowned', here referring to the ice cream which is drowned in coffee. Use good quality ice cream.*

4 small scoops chocolate ice cream
4 small scoops vanilla ice cream
freshly made espresso coffee

**serves 4**

Divide the ice cream between 4 chilled coffee cups, top up with the hot coffee and serve.

# ginger and lemon tisane

*This lightly spiced tisane has a wonderful cleansing effect on the body – an ideal start to the day.*

5 cm piece of fresh ginger, peeled

2 stalks lemongrass

4 teaspoons honey

1 lemon, sliced

**serves 4**

Thinly slice the ginger and cut each lemongrass stalk in half crossways, then lengthways. Put the ginger and lemongrass into cups, then add the honey and a slice of lemon. Top up with boiling water and serve.

# champagne cocktails

*There is something decidedly decadent about a glass of fizz in the morning, so if you're going to treat yourself to brunch, why not totally spoil yourself with one of these cocktails.*

### campari fizz

6 shots of Campari

3 teaspoons caster sugar

1 bottle chilled sparkling wine, 750 ml

**serves 6**

Pour the Campari into champagne flutes and sweeten each with ½ teaspoon sugar. Top up with sparkling wine and serve.

### peach bellini

3 ripe peaches

1 bottle chilled Prosecco or sparkling wine, 750 ml

**serves 6**

Peel the peaches by plunging them into boiling water for 30 seconds. Refresh them under cold water and peel off the skin. Cut in half, remove the stone and chop the flesh.

Put the peaches into a blender, add a small amount of Prosecco and process to a purée. Pour into glasses, top up with the remaining Prosecco and serve.

### mimosa

6 blood oranges or ordinary oranges

1 bottle chilled sparkling wine, 750 ml

**serves 6**

Squeeze the oranges and divide the juice between 6 glasses. Top up with wine and serve.

# cool drinks

*Fruit and yoghurt drinks are packed full of goodness and vitality and could almost be served as a meal in themselves. When really ripe mangoes are unavailable, canned mango purée, available from Asian stores, makes a great alternative.*

## raspberry and rosewater lassi

250 g raspberries

4 tablespoons rosewater

300 ml natural yoghurt

2–3 tablespoons honey

12 ice cubes

**serves 4**

Put all the ingredients in a blender. Blend to a purée and serve.

## mango, coconut and passionfruit shake

1 large mango, peeled,
or 300 ml mango purée

6 large passionfruit,
or 150 ml passionfruit juice

200 ml coconut milk

12 ice cubes

**serves 4**

Cut the mango flesh away from the stone. Coarsely chop the flesh and put into a blender. Cut the passionfruit in half and scoop the seeds into a sieve placed over a bowl. Use a spoon to press down the seeds and extract all the juice. Add the juice, coconut milk and ice cubes to the blender and purée until smooth and creamy.

# index